I0457032

"GIRL TURNED WOMAN BEFORE HER TIME"

A Story of Survival

Hebrews 10:35-36

[35] So do not throw away your confidence; it will be richly rewarded.

[36] You need to persevere so that when you have done the will of God, you will receive what he has promised.

"GIRL TURNED WOMAN BEFORE HER TIME"

A Story of Survival

Hebrews 10:35-36

[35] So do not throw away your confidence; it will be richly rewarded.

[36] You need to persevere so that when you have done the will of God, you will receive what he has promised.

LINDA ANN MILLER

Copyright © 2025 by Linda Ann Miller

All rights reserved. No part of this book may be used or reproduced by any means, graphic, electronic, or mechanical, including photocopying, recording, taping, or by any information storage retrieval system, without the written permission of the publisher except in the case of brief quotations embodied in critical articles and reviews.

ISBN: 979-8-218-69552-1

Unless otherwise indicated, Scripture taken from the New King James Version®. Copyright © 1982 by Thomas Nelson. Used by permission. All rights reserved.

Design Director: Dawn Harvey-Owens

Published by:
UPH. Div., Maximized Productions Publishing Division
6715 Suitland Road
Morningside, Maryland 20746
(301) 420-1460
www.maximizedproductions.com/publishing/

Printed in the USA

Contents

Forward

My story has been locked up inside me all my life and tucked away in the caverns of my heart and mind. Because of my past, I have been changed, and the change has been evident. Without my story, I would not be who I am today, and that person is Linda Miller.

Over the years, I have l learned "Who" Linda Miller is and what the Lord had in store for me even from the womb. The time had come that I wrote it down so that all the little girls in the world who have been through a myriad of abuses in their lives can know and understand that there is HOPE outside of the abuse. And that HOPE has a name... Jesus Christ. With Him, ALL things are possible (Matthew 19:26)!

I dedicate this book to my three beautiful children, Robert, Gregory and Tiffany. They have always known me as "Mom". I now want them to know me as a woman who has fought great adversity and struggled to survive insurmountable odds and become the person God in Heaven had always intended me to be.

Life gives us all sorts of things, some good and some bad. I want them always to know that no matter what happens in our lives or what fears come our way, we can have peace because our Lord and Savior, Jesus Christ, has overcome the world. (John 16:33).

I hope you see JESUS and that He is glorified through my story; we can do nothing without Him. To all the women reading this book, I pray that the little girl who has always been inside you finds peace and the love you so richly deserve. That love is found in Jesus Christ, and He alone is the One that takes what the enemy meant for evil, and He turns it around for good (Genesis 50:20). My prayer is that you will allow the Lord to do just that, and you find inner healing in your life.

God sets us up sometimes by giving us only a piece of the picture at a time. We would probably have been scared to death if we had seen the whole picture! Then, when we say yes to Him, He opens it up wide for us to see all He wants us to do. It's important to know that the Lord does not look at what man looks at. Man looks at the outward appearance, but the Lord looks at the heart (1 Samuel 16:7b).

The revelation awaits an appointed time; it speaks of the end and will not prove false. Though it lingers, please wait for it. It will certainly come and will not be delayed (Habakkuk 2:3).

When we experience good things in our lives, such as when the Lord provides for us, or we get victory in something, we are usually ready and WILLING to tell people what the Lord has done, and He receives glory through this. However, when we experience something horrific that we wished would have never happened, we protect ourselves because we want to protect our image.

We are molded by what we experience because of our circumstances. We don't want anyone to KNOW what happened because it may cause people to look at us differently. When we do this, the Lord CANNOT receive any glory, which should not be. I believe that HE gets greater glory when it borders on the impossible, when no one else can solve the problem, or no one else can bring you out. Do you not know that your body is a temple of the Holy Spirit, who is in you, whom you have received from God? You are not your own; you were bought at a price. Therefore, honor God with your body (1 Corinthians 6:19-20).

We don't have to protect our image because we belong to God; HE will protect our image, and the image others will see is Christ!

While in college, I wrote the following on my way back from Tennessee. I had to do a presentation for my class, so I read this as a dramatic reading for the class. I followed it up by playing the song **Concrete Angel by Martina McBride**. There wasn't a dry eye in the whole class! I had it notarized. This little girl was deep inside me, waiting to come out. Take a few minutes to listen to the song.

Little Girl Turned Woman
A Story of Survival

As a young girl looks into the mirror, she sees a small girl turned woman before her time. Her mind cannot interpret the actions happening to her that should not be! She tries to reason in her mind-- with no success. Why? Daddy, Why? This doesn't feel right–normal, it's not. How I know this, I do not know. Maybe my heart is trying to show me. I don't know where to go or which way to turn. What do I do? I long for security and peace. I feel so alone with my secrets and shame— alone with no way to work them out. Where is God in all this, I wonder? Not realizing it, He's always there right by my side. Man has free will, and sometimes, he chooses the wrong things. It changes my world! Who am I? Who will I become? I feel so isolated and afraid—I am forced to become the protector—How do I do that? I need to be protected from this twisted, dysfunctional life that I find myself in! I am screaming, and no one can hear me. Someone, please look at me and recognize the situation that I am in! Please get involved so I can be spared this trauma of abuse. I am forced to do things that are unthinkable for a small girl, things that I cannot even utter— SSSSHHH! It's our secret, I am told--Daddy No! I scream in my spirit, why, Daddy, why? I even realize this is not right—where is Mommy in all this? The abusive behavior *itself does not cause the most trauma, but it is the response to the behavior that leaves me scarred—invisible scars—no one can see the wounds that are bleeding—they refuse to heal! My needs, longings and opinions don't matter— Why? I'm important! My desires are clothed in hiding as my spirit is chipped away little by little! The center of my heart is yearning for something better than this evil I found myself in. In the face of all that is wrong, a flicker of hope begs to be turned into a flame of spiritual rest. I know that I can survive— and I do! Thank God!*

~~~

For I know the plans I have for you declares the Lord, plans to prosper you and not harm you, plans to give you a hope and a future (**Jeremiah 29:11**).

Come and listen, all you who fear God, let me tell you what he has done for me. (**Psalm 66:16**).

Blended Together

My mother Karen divorced my father, Frank Fortenberry and married my stepfather, Earl Ouellette when my sister Mary was three, I was two, and our sister Nancy was just one. My mother had three more children, Earl Jr., Edward and Elinore, and we became a blended family over the next several years and began our lives together. My stepfather Earl had three children from a previous marriage, Roger, Dennis and Rose, with whom we kept in contact over the years. Rose is now deceased; I was able to go and see her just before she died.

I do not remember my biological father, Frank, very well, although I did have some minor contact with him over the years when he was in town. I didn't feel like I had a very close relationship with him. When I was older, my mother told me that my dad, Frank, had been a gambler and that he often left us with no money for the necessities of life, such as milk and food. I don't understand why a father doesn't take responsibility for his family and allows other things to take precedence in their lives to the detriment of losing his own family.

My stepfather Earl was in the military before he married my mom, so he always had stories to tell. He had been in the Korean War, and he would tell us kids about how he was a prisoner of war and how he was shot and lost one of his kidneys. I know that war can be very detrimental to a person's life and change it forever. He made it out of the war alive with God's great mercy. It seemed he was unscathed by the war on the outside, but the inside was marred, and no one could see. Those scars began to unfold in his life, and they touched him and his entire family. They would never be the same as those scars manifested in various ways.

My mother, Karen, had been a homemaker most of her life, but years later, she went to work in a factory when my dad's plant went into closure. We were left at home with Dad when she went to work.

My mother was an only child and lost both of her parents in death at an early age, so she was raised by her grandmother, Tilley. I remember visiting Grandma Tilly's house to spend the night with her. She would give me a couple of quarters to dust the furniture and help her around the house. The thought of someone giving me two quarters was more than I could imagine! At night, we would walk along the long corridor, and we would go up the winding stairway to her bedroom, and before bed, she would remove all the hair pins and undo her long wavy hair and let me brush it for her before she would tuck me into bed in the room next to hers. I felt loved by her.

In the morning, I loved being in her kitchen and helping her with breakfast, and I treasured every minute of it. It seemed normal, something I did not know or had experienced in my young life. I remember when my Grandma Tilley died, she had left me and each one of my siblings $1,000.00 in her will. When I turned 21 years old, I was able to receive it.

I always considered the family I grew up in to be at the lower economic level because we never seemed to have enough money and didn't seem to have half as much as others; however, I suppose we had more than some. Maybe it's because Mom and Dad spent a lot of money on alcohol.

That Fateful Day

Living in Detroit at the time, my earliest memory is from the age of 4; I see myself standing in the front living area, looking up at my mother with my brown hair hanging in my face and telling her what had just happened to me. I don't remember my words; I remember telling her what happened. I don't recall what she said to me in response to what I just told her, but I know from that fateful day I never "told" again, and I began keeping secrets, and those secrets started forming my young life.

I was being forced down a long, dark and twisted road that I should not have had to travel, but travel I did. I was the one who primarily raised my siblings from an early age, which was a responsibility no child should have. I found myself becoming the protector of all my younger siblings. No matter how hard I tried to protect my siblings, I could not succeed. I never had the opportunity to enjoy being a child because I had been forced to behave like an adult and had no idea how to do that. Responsibilities were placed on me by my parents that I had no idea how to handle. When I failed, I was beaten and punished. I remember one time I was sent to my room and told not to come out. I was so fearful; I messed in my pants and then spanked because of it.

There were so many role reversals which came into play in my young life. An example of this was when my father was drunk one time, and he was crying and telling me that he was going to die. I sat on the edge of his bed where he was lying, and he kept telling me over and over that he was going to die. There I sat, holding his hand and telling him that everything was going to be ok. As a child, I didn't know what to do. I don't know where Mom was probably at work at the time. There I was, comforting him when he should have been the one comforting me. He finally drifted off to sleep and was I freed for a moment... until the next time.

Generational Curses/ Family Background

Many generational Curses were woven into my life with no way to stop them. One thing I did was excel in school and fervently tried to be perceived as normal. I found myself using coping mechanisms without realizing it. I believe that excelling in school provided me with some kind of control and normalcy in my life. It was my way of forgetting what was happening at home.

I never wanted to have any friends over to my home because of what they might encounter while they were there. I had no real friends in my so-called childhood. True loneliness had settled into my heart from an early age, and it would be many years before I would be released from that feeling and be replaced with love.

My Parents had slowly become alcoholics, and things around the house were out of control most of the time. They were both trying to cover up what was happening behind closed doors. I feel that my mother was trying to cover up what was happening to her children. Everything looked "normal" outside the home, but pure evil was going on inside the home. The home's exterior was pristine, the flower beds were clear of weeds, and the vegetable garden was always tended by us children. On the outside, everything appeared wonderful but inside was quite a different story.

As a parent and a mother, I don't understand what makes individuals do the unthinkable. What makes a person do something so inconceivable that it changed my life and left me scarred? These scars had become a part of me; they were so ingrained within me, and I had no idea how to have these scars healed. It would be years before I found the answer. I was in survival mode and looking for some normalcy.

There was abuse of ALL gametes (physical, emotional, psychological, and yes, even sexual abuse) in my life with no way to stop it and no way to be free from it all. There had to be something better. The Word of God says *You were taught about your former way of life, to put off your old self, which is being corrupted by its deceitful desires; to be made new in the attitude of your minds; and to put on the new self, created to be like God in true righteousness and holiness (Ephesians 4:22-24).*

When my family was still living in Detroit, I got into trouble and wasn't sure what I did. My parents punished me and made me get down on my knees on the cold kitchen floor and fold my hands like I was praying and repeat over and over, "I will not be bossy" "I will not be bossy." They made me do this until I cried uncontrollably. As young as I was (about 7), I thought to myself, I am expected to watch and care for the other children and then get into trouble when I do. I couldn't understand what they expected of me. I was just a child.

All my siblings struggled in their own way; we were trying to survive the turmoil behind closed doors. No one knew what was going on in our home. While living in Detroit, I attended a Catholic School from Kindergarten through 3rd grade. My sisters Mary and Nancy were in Special Education, and all the kids always picked on them; I found myself trying to protect them. In later years, my brother Edward had difficulty staying out of trouble and was placed in a boys' home at a young age. I remember going and visiting him and wondering why he couldn't come home. The abuse had affected him as well.

When I was eight years old and entering the fourth grade, we moved from Detroit to Taylor, and I thought things would get better, but they didn't. I never knew what to expect from day to day. I don't know why I thought things could be different just because we lived elsewhere. I guess I just hoped that they would be. School was very difficult now because I had gone from a private school to a public one, which was very different. It took me that whole year to adjust to the new ways of learning.

At home, I remember an incident when some of us kids were sitting at the kitchen table, and I believe there was a bit of arguing going on between us. Suddenly, my father came out of his room in a wild rage and started yelling at us. He blamed me because of what was going on. His arms began swinging and hitting me, and he just kept on yelling at me. I don't remember what the other kids were doing; I remember him. I don't even remember how it ended or what he did after he calmed down. He probably went back to bed.

My family did not have very much family cohesion. We each tried to make our own way; I believe we were all just trying to survive. I don't remember spending time together, just doing family stuff. My parents seemed to have their daily agenda, and I felt they were worried about where their next drink would come from.

I believe that we kids were sort of close in a dysfunctional way. We were trying to survive the day's turmoil. I guess we had loyalty to one another; we kept things to ourselves and away from friends or family. We just wanted to be perceived as normal. The only activity that I can remember as a child growing up was my mother would make a birthday cake for my birthday; however, I don't remember any particular present. The only present I remember is that we four girls got an Easy Bake Oven for Christmas one year when I was in the third grade, and we had to share it.

At times, I felt like I didn't get enough to eat. Even at my young age, I knew six children were in the home and food was expensive. I recall when my mother and father bought two porter house steaks for themselves and only gave us a bite or two. We were never able to have one for ourselves. As a parent now, I would never have thought of doing such a thing. If I could not afford steaks for everyone, then no one would get one. I would, however, give it to my children before myself because that is what a mother does.

I remember cooking at an early age and standing on a stool to do the dishes. I always had more than enough chores to do regularly and never seemed to be able to get everything done. My mother canned and froze everything that she could. Once, she brought live chickens home from the farm and cut their heads off in the backyard. After they stopped running around, we kids had to bring them inside, put them in scalding water, and pluck all the feathers out so they could be put in the freezer. We made homemade jelly and had to help with all the canning. It was not easy growing up in this family.

The only family vacations we took were driving up north and visiting family. I can remember looking at the colorful trees and noticing the scenery that I saw all around me. I was in awe at the beauty of it all! I thought there had to be more than what I knew or the life I was living.

Alcohol began to touch us all and attached itself to several of us. I believe children do and say what they see and hear. Growing up, there was not much flexibility in my home; what mom and dad said went. Mom would always say, "Wait until your father gets home." She never took the time to discipline us or try to get matters in hand until they had escalated and were out of control. The discipline was strict; I was spanked with a belt by the hands that were supposed to protect me. My mom would pull me up by my hair so severely that my head would be sore for days. I could not imagine doing that to my children now. God help those that do!

There were no negotiations in the family. We kids rarely had a say about what happened in the home because we just lived there. I don't remember any specific rules growing up; I just did what I was told. Chaos reigned in my home. Proverbs 25:28 a man without self-control is like a city broken into and left without walls. Change was difficult for my family; anything that was out of the ordinary seemed to upset the apple cart, so to speak. Everything had to be routine or else. At times, everything was disorganized, and as much as we kids tried to do everything together, we would fail. We were only children! We should not have had to worry about such things in our young lives.

Court Day

I remember going to court with my mother, father, and sister, Nancy. I am unsure if Nancy remembers this, but it has been etched into my mind for all these years. My sister Mary was there also. I don't know how, but someone reported that our father had abused my sister, Nancy, and that is why we were in court. I was in the waiting room waiting for them to come out of court, and when they did, my father was yelling and called Nancy a liar over and over. I don't remember seeing her face; I only saw him. I knew that Nancy was not lying and that it was all true. I was so frightened, and I knew that she was also. I don't recall seeing my mom's face or what she may have said. My baby sister Elinore had to go to foster care for an unknown time, and the rest of us went home. Our father had to go and spend some time in a mental hospital called Elouise in Westland, and I remember we kids had to go and visit him, something that I didn't want to do. As a child, I thought, how come mom never did anything to protect us? I remember walking around on the grounds of this facility and not wanting to be there. I don't remember any interactions with my father while there; maybe I had blocked it out of my mind and heart, but I don't know. He was allowed to come home again after he served his time there. I don't know how long he had to be there, but he came home, and my mother allowed him to do so.

I don't understand why some adults end up the way they do. My parents had responsible people in their lives; at least, I thought so. I believe that the choices that we make in life can be very detrimental to our way of life. My parents made bad choices and allowed their decisions to sway them from going in the right direction. Unfortunately, those choices and decisions touched their children's lives, and we are all a product of them.

Major parenting roles were transferred to me. I had no idea how to do this in my young life. I felt alone most of the time, even though the house was full of people. Even in adulthood, I felt at times that I was alone, even in a room full of people. I have been a loner most of my life. I believe that was how I protected myself because that was what I was used to doing.

While raising my children, I always tried my best to make them feel like they belonged and were important members of the family. I had learned what NOT to do. I had always provided my children with love and acceptance, not only with words but with actions. If I can continue to be successful with my children, they will be fulfilled in their lives and be upstanding members of society with much to offer others. My children have not always agreed with me, but that's ok. I love them unconditionally and will always hold them close to my heart and uphold them in my prayers.

I have made many mistakes and had to learn from the "Master" how to be a mother and "How" to love my children. Everything I learned, I learned from the Lord Almighty.

I had found in my life that those things that were meant for destruction can and were turned around for good. That is God's way. The word of God says, "You intended to harm me, but God intended it for good to accomplish what is now being done, the saving of many lives (Genesis 50:20). God's word never fails!

Hiding Under Cover

At the age of sixteen, I began using drugs and alcohol. I was trying to hide the shame I felt, the loneliness, the guilt, the feelings I had that no one could see or even understand. I could not let anyone see who Linda was and what I had found myself engulfed in. There had to be an answer, but I didn't know what it was.

I met my future husband, Robert, as a junior in High School, and I thought I had finally found out what Love was. He was such a "Fox," I thought. I was blinded by physical love. I allowed myself to be enticed into having sex with him because this is what I thought was "normal." There was no enjoyment for me at all; it was over very quickly; he got what he wanted, and I just retreated more into the recesses of my heart where I could hide all that happened as I usually did or as I was trained to do because of what I endured in my life at home.

Shortly after meeting Robert, my family home was foreclosed, and my parents and five siblings had to live in a motel for some time. I was sixteen and had just received a promotion at a local grocery store where I worked, and I didn't want to lose my job. I had the opportunity to go live with a family friend and her family and finish my senior year of High school. I began my new life free from the things that seemed to haunt me. At least, I thought so at the time.

Theresa taught me so many things while I was living there. I learned how to take care of my finances and myself. I was living in a home that seemed to have peace and tranquility. There was laughter and love, a different kind of love I had not experienced up to that point. Life was different. Theresa saved me from the turmoil I was living in at home, even though she had no idea. It was a blessing that our home was lost to foreclosure because it was my way out. I lived there until after I graduated in 1980 when I worked and supported myself. I had escaped, so I thought. I remember telling my counselor that I felt like I abandoned my siblings. She replied, "You didn't abandon them, you were trying to save your life."

After graduation, my cousin Sue and I moved into a friend's home, where I worked at a local nursing home and lived until Sue moved out and married a man named Muriel. We both had to pay for our things, such as rent, food, and toiletries. I valued my friendship with my cousin because we both experienced some of the same things. We did many things together and trusted one another, which was always hard for me to trust people. We had formed such a bond, and I still value it today even though we live apart. After Sue moved out, I continued learning how to manage my money, pay my bills and care for myself. I felt so alone and like something was missing in my life. It would be years before I found out what that was. Shortly after Sue moved out, I moved into Robert's family home until we got married at 20 (August 27, 1982).

Married and moved to Colorado

Robert and I were both out of work, and his aunt said we could come to Colorado with her and her husband, but we would need to get married first. We had been going together for 5 years, so we quickly planned a wedding, not realizing what we were getting ourselves into. I wore Roberts's sister's wedding dress, which fit me perfectly, and we held the ceremony in her backyard. There was a party afterwards, with a beer keg, and Robert's mom made us a beautiful wedding cake. I was still trying to be perceived as "normal."

Two days after the wedding, we moved to Colorado Springs and were there for about 2 years. Still keep secrets and protecting myself.

I did not know "how" to be a wife or "how" to continue to be normal, but somehow, I managed to portray normalcy in my day-to-day life. Colorado was just beautiful; I was fascinated with the beauty of it all. When I went to the mountains, I felt like I was in a different atmosphere, away from all my pain and uncertainty, until I had to descend into the city again.

We had our trials in our marriage that first year; we almost didn't make it. We lived with his aunt and uncle for a short time before we moved into a small trailer. I remember when we were struggling financially in the middle of wintertime, and we found ourselves with no heat. Our trailer was heated by propane, and we also used it to cook with it. We didn't have enough money to fill the propane tank, so we had no heat for about a month. It was so frigid in the trailer; I would curl up on the couch and cover up with an electric blanket to stay warm. It was so cold in the home that I could see my breath. We even had to go over to the neighbors to cook our food.

This was something that I had endured growing up as a child; we were without electricity or hot water many times. We had to heat our water on the stove before we kids could take a bath. By the grace of God, I have never allowed my children to be without the necessities of life because a bill could not be paid.

Several people lived with us over the two years while we were in Colorado. Hindsight, I know that this wasn't a good idea. There are enough stressors in a new marriage without adding someone else into the picture. While we were living in the trailer, a friend moved in, and because of him, we were evicted and had to find another place to live. We ended up moving into an apartment. My brother-in-law Paul and his wife Diane came to Colorado to see if they could find work. They were staying with us in our one-bedroom apartment; they were struggling with their marriage. They couldn't find work, so they moved back to Michigan and later divorced. I always had a really good relationship with my sister-in-law, and I knew I would miss her terribly in my life. I now have her as a friend on Facebook, and I can see her family pictures.

I worked in a nursing home while in Colorado, became a certified nursing assistant (CENA), and made a difference in many seniors' lives. I felt that I had grown as a person as I learned new skills and could implement those skills not only among my peers but with the seniors I cared for. I remember one instance when a senior was choking in the dining room, and I performed the Heimlich maneuver on him and saved him from choking to death. I felt so grateful that I was there when he needed me. I had so much love to give that had been bottled up within me for many years.

My parents came to Colorado for a visit and fell in love with the state of Colorado so much that they decided to move there. My father had breathing difficulties due to a lifetime of smoking; the air was drier in Colorado, so it made it a bit easier for him to breathe. My parents knew my husband and I planned to move back to Michigan when we learned we were expecting our first child. It was strange to leave them again, but I had no regrets moving away from them at the time. It wasn't until many years later that I would feel different in my heart.

When we got back to Michigan, I was 4 months pregnant, and the Lord had given me the wisdom to stop drinking and doing drugs without me realizing it. I thank God for that! I was still keeping secrets, still trying to be normal. What was normal? I didn't have any idea. My emotional, psychological and spiritual scars would not be healed until many years later. I had made many mistakes in my life that formed my life.

My Heart Transplant

On January 10, 1988, I went to church and gave my heart to the Lord. The message's title was "A Time for Change" I went to the altar that morning, not realizing what I was doing. I wept like a baby as I knelt at the altar that morning. I spoke no tangible words, but my heart was opened to the One who could and did change my life. The precious blood of Jesus Christ was applied to my heart, and I was changed forever! I didn't comprehend or realize what happened until I left the church that day. I was raised Catholic and did not understand what had just happened; I just knew something did! The feeling I had was like none other I had ever experienced in my entire life. I felt like I was walking 4 feet off the floor. I now knew that God loved me. *God so loved the world that he gave his one and only Son, that whoever believes in him shall not perish but have eternal life* (John 3:16).

There was such joy in my heart, and I couldn't stop smiling. It was like a great burden had been lifted off me, and I was free. *"Come to me, all you who are weary and burdened, and I will give you rest. Take my yoke upon you and learn from me, for I am gentle and humble in heart, and you will find rest for your souls. ³⁰ For my yoke is easy and my burden is light."* (Matthew 11:28-30). I will never forget that as I knelt at my bed that first night and prayed to God, I felt like there were butterflies within me. I knew that God was with me and that it was His very presence that I was feeling.

Two days later, I was invited to a prayer meeting; I didn't even know what a prayer meeting was, but I went anyway. That night, I was baptized with the Holy Ghost and had the evidence of speaking in tongues; I would never be the same. What was this, I thought? *When the day of Pentecost came, they were all together in one place. Suddenly, a sound like the blowing of a violent wind came from heaven and filled the whole house where they were sitting. They saw what seemed to be tongues of fire that separated and came to rest on each of them. All of them were filled with the Holy Spirit and began to speak in other tongues as the Spirit enabled them* (Acts 2:1-4).

My life changed drastically and has continued throughout my entire life. There is so much of God's love, and He wants to have a personal relationship with each one of us. He is Omnipresent, Omnipotent (all-powerful) and Omniscient (all-knowing). I felt that the presence of the Lord was overwhelming to me; I had never in my life felt that kind of love.

Sometimes, God can do more when individuals don't have any preconceived ideas about how something should be or how something should be handled. HE knows what HE is doing. We need to let go and let God. From the Lord comes deliverance; may your blessing be on your people. Promise of Restoration: *Call me and I will answer you and show you great and unsearchable things you do not know. Nevertheless, I will bring health and healing to it; I will heal my people and will let them enjoy abundant peace and security* (Jeremiah 33:3, 6).

I was instantly delivered from drugs and alcohol, and I never smoked cigarettes again. I had smoked for 8 years and couldn't get free from them until the day I met the Lord! It would still be years before my unseen scars would be healed. I had become very good at hiding the scars that had become a part of me. I remember getting all my secular concert t-shirts out, cutting them into shreds and then throwing them into the dumpster. I didn't want any part of that kind of life any longer.

The more I served the Lord in my life, the more I began to experience even more generational curses that began to be peeled away. An example of this was my mother screamed at me and my siblings all our lives; it was so entrenched in my life. I found myself doing the same thing. I was so desperate to have this reversed in my life that it took the Lord's power to free me from this. I wrote in my journal about it; I prayed about it; I sought the Lord about it. Finally, I was free from this generational curse. This was the first of many things reversed in my life, and the Lord continued working on me.

And we know that in all things, God works for the good of those who love him and have been called according to his purpose (Romans 8:28). We may not know this right away, but it is something that we learn over time. Everyone learns over time. For He has rescued us from the dominion of darkness and brought us into the kingdom of the Son He loves, in whom we have redemption, the forgiveness of sins (Col 1:13).

All my mistakes had been forgiven, and now I just needed the Lord to help me **forgive myself.**

My Children/Grandchildren

When our first-born son, Robert Earl, came into the world, we lived at Robert's mother's home. Labor pains began in the evening, and we finally made our way to the hospital for delivery. Robert Earl DeVore was born about 14 hours after the labor pains began. It was a difficult delivery, and I had to have the placenta delivered by the doctor's hands and, therefore, had to have a blood transfusion. He was 9.5 pounds and looked like he was about 3 months old. He had a head full of dark hair and was just beautiful! I thought that he looked a lot like his daddy. I was overjoyed beyond belief when I held him in my arms for the first time. Robert's mom, Jean, has always been a good support for me. The bond that was forming between her and me will last a lifetime! I don't believe I could have managed without her by my side.

When my son Robert was born, it enabled me to experience such love for another human being. I wanted to protect him and love him no matter what. My instincts kicked in because I had no idea HOW to love someone so intensely. He grew very quickly and was so smart.

When he was two years old, we moved into our apartment and started our family life. It was not easy; we struggled with finances all the time. We both worked opposite shifts to make ends meet. We rarely had to use a babysitter, which I was happy about. Robb began walking at just 8 months old, and this caused his legs to bow quite a bit. I was concerned, so I scheduled him to see an orthopedic surgeon to ensure his legs were developing correctly. After the testing, we were told that his legs were developing fine and that there was nothing to worry about. This was such a great relief to me and his dad. No one is given a manual on child rearing; we learn as we go.

My precious son had difficulties in his life as he grew up, as we all do. I made mistakes, but I tried to learn from them. We took him to a Christian counselor, whom he wasn't happy about, but we thought it was the best decision at the time. Everyone makes decisions in their lives, even children, as they grow up, and we all live by those decisions. My son has his testimony about his life, so I will not go into more detail. I will say that I loved him through all that he went through and always will. The things he went through affected not only him but also me, and the rest of the family. I always asked God to help and guide me in everything I did. I have always covered him in prayer and would always pray for his future and his family that God would give him one day. Still today, I continue to put him into God's mighty hands and believe in great things in his life. Robb is an adult now and has been with the love of his life, Angela, for many years. They have a beautiful son named Antonio, my grandson.

Long before Antonio was born, Angela moved in with our family because she was forced out of her home. I have not been allowed to be a part of their lives for unknown reasons, but I pray that one day restoration can be obtained so that we can be joined again. I fervently pray for all 3 of them and stand on God's Word. Train up a child in the way he should go; when he is old, he will not depart from it (Proverbs 22:6). I am a praying mother, and there is nothing stronger than that except God.

My Second Born – Open Heart Surgery

My labor pains began while I was at work. I was working as a private CENA for an elderly couple in their home. Once my husband picked me up we made our way to the hospital. While I was walking into the hospital, I was having contractions: I had to stop several times and breathe through the contractions before I was taken to a hospital room. I was hooked up to a monitor and then unhooked and taken to the delivery room. Within minutes, my second son was born, and he weighed 8.6 pounds. We had not given him a name until a couple of days later, and I knew something wasn't quite right. I wanted to try to nurse him, so the nurse assisted me; however, he was not able to latch on. The nurse told me later that they were going to give him some oxygen because he was having difficulty with his breathing and was going to keep him in the nursery. The next day, I was told that he was still having difficulty breathing, so they were going to fly him to Mott's Children's Hospital in Ann Arbor, Michigan. I stood at the window of my hospital room alone and looked out the window as they loaded him into the ambulance helicopter. I felt helpless and scared and didn't know what would happen from that point. I watched as the helicopter lifted off the roof of the hospital and flew out sight with tears streaming down my face. My husband met me at the hospital, and we drove to the hospital to meet our son. He was in the hospital for 5 days until they could get him on room oxygen and allowed him to come home. We named him Gregory Adam DeVore.

Four weeks later, Greg had to be rushed to the hospital because he kept crying and seemed to be turning blue. A friend who happened to be a nurse came over and told us to call the hospital and let them know that we were coming. Greg slept the whole way there. I believe that the Lord comforted him as we drove to the hospital. Greg had a heart catheterization done on Friday and was diagnosed with Tetralogy of Fallot. He had a hole in his heart, and an artery was too narrow. On Monday, God took us through open heart surgery with our son Greg at just 5 weeks old to patch the hole and widen the artery. I didn't know what fear was until then. The hospital staff had to let us know of all the possibilities that could happen with the surgery, including death.

When they were taking my son through the doors into the operating room, I had to stay outside the doors. My pastor at the time told me that Jesus went through the doors with Greg and He would take care of him. Hours later, when he finally came back out, I could only get a glimpse of him because they had to get him into recovery and get him stabilized. It would be two more hours before I could see him again. He was so small and was all stretched out with machines all around him and tubes protruding from his little body. My insides were trembling, and tears were streaming from my eyes. I prayed to God, who could take care of everything.

Many prayed for him over the next days to follow. The Lord made it possible for me to be at the hospital daily and even provided the finances and the rides to the hospital while my husband was working. Friends took care of my son Robb while I was away. I saw the hand of God every day on my son Greg as they took him off the vent and removed tubes from him. I finally got to hold him in my arms. I experienced such joy in finally holding him; I never wanted to let him go. I grew so much spiritually and mentally through this experience, and I learned to trust the Lord more and more.

Greg had to have open heart surgery again when he was just 16 years old. He had to have some of the muscles near his heart removed because it was pressing up against the artery of his heart. It was such a contrast between infancy and young adulthood. Greg doesn't remember when he was a baby, but he did when he was sixteen. The only way we can grow up is by going through difficult circumstances. But remember…they are only circumstances. Jesus said himself in John 16:33. I have told you these things so you may have peace in me. In this world, you will have trouble. But take heart: I have overcome the world. Let the circumstances come, and we can have peace no matter what comes our way. Greg is now an adult married to the love of his life, Lauren. They have two beautiful children, Summer and Parker. When Lauren was little, her mom and dad, our friends, would visit us at our home, and Lauren would play with my daughter Tiffany. It is awesome that the Lord knew Lauren and Greg would marry one day.

God gives a Daughter

We were blessed a third time on July 18, 1994, with our daughter Tiffany Marie, and our family was complete. I was told after an ultrasound that I was pregnant with a girl, but it wasn't until she was born, and the nurse said it was a girl that I was overcome with even more love for her. She was just beautiful and weighed 8.2 pounds. My best friend Kathy was there the next day. She saw her and immediately fell in love with her. Kathy became Tiffany's godmother soon after.

I had always wanted a mother-daughter relationship because I had never had one with my mother. I still remember the day that I realized I would never have that relationship with my mother in my life, and I came to terms with it. Tiffany looks a lot like I did when I was younger, and she has the same personality I have. I guess that can be a good thing, or maybe not. Our family was complete with two beautiful sons and now a beautiful daughter. Tiffany married the love of her life, KC, and they were expecting their first child. However, soon after conception, she lost the baby. It was a devastating time for them both and me as well. This would have been my first grandchild, but now I needed to wait until I got to heaven to see Kennedy. Tiffany later had a daughter named Scarlett. When Scarlett was just 4 years old, KC died tragically. Tiffany was now a widow with a 4-year-old daughter to raise. My heart was broken for her, and I made sure that I was available for her to help her with this tragic event in her life. She would never be the same, but she was a strong young woman. She had watched me when insurmountable odds would come my way and saw that I always sought the Lord to help me, and so did she. I am so very proud of the young woman she has become. She has grown so much in every way. She now has a wonderful man named Doug in her life and he treats Tiffany like a queen and loves my granddaughter like his own daughter.

Secret Revealed

I had been married for many years, and there was something that my husband did not know about me, something that I had gone through in my life, something that I buried deep and didn't allow anyone to know about. It was to protect myself, I thought.

During a revival at church, my life changed. How many of you know that if nobody knows something in your life… there is always someone who knows!! God knows everything, and He reveals it in his time. Daniel 2:22 He reveals deep and hidden things; He knows what lies in darkness, and light dwells in Him.

After the church service, the Evangelist and the pastor's wife came off the stage and approached me. He began to tell me what my father had put me through for years and that it was not my fault. All I could do was weep uncontrollably. Someone DID KNOW what had happened to me for so many years, and it was NOT my fault. I was validated. I spent two more nights at the altar before I went home and told my husband what had happened to me **(for 12 years).**

I sat on the edge of the bed weeping uncontrollably and told my husband what was revealed at church through the minister after the service ended. He asked me if I wanted to talk about it, and I said no, not right now. He never asked me again. Maybe he was trying to pretend that it never happened. Perhaps he didn't know exactly what to do or say in this situation. Sometimes "Words" are not needed.

People think that to support someone, they need to say something. Sometimes, we need someone to be present and provide no words. Sometimes, we don't know what to say, and our presence says everything. When the Lord resides in our hearts, He makes our hearts known to others, instilling peace.

Job 2:13 says they sat on the ground with him for seven days and nights. No one said a word to Job, for they saw that his suffering was too great for words. We can't always fix someone in their sorrow, but we can be present. I needed him to be present and sit with me without speaking. Silence can be productive and provide a loving presence in another person's life. I buried my pain again.

Forgiveness Came

Ephesians 4:32 Be kind and compassionate to one another, forgiving each other just as in Christ God forgave you. I forgave my parents in my heart for what they put me through for so many years. It's important to know that it was not for them that I did this; it was for me. It was so that I could continue to be healed and transformed. If we cannot forgive others, how can we expect God to forgive us?? I did not do this alone; I did it with the help of the Lord!

Romans 12:2 Do not conform any longer to the pattern of this world but be transformed by the renewing of your mind. Then, you will be able to test and approve what God's good and perfect will is.

When my father was near death, I told my mother to make sure that she had the hospital chaplain visit him to share the gospel with him. I wanted to make sure that he knew the Lord before he died. I remember standing at his casket after his service, and all I could do was cry as I looked at my father. He looked so frail, and I was remembering how I felt as a child, wishing that I had felt protected, loved, and cherished as a daughter. I was crying for what might have been.

When my mother passed away, I went to Colorado to help my brother Earl clean the house and pack up the few things that had to be shipped back to Michigan. While there, I thought of when my mother was visiting me at home, and I was sitting at the table with her. I was in college then and read her one of the papers I had written for class. I believe she finally realized that her daughter was doing well and said she was proud of me. While I was cleaning her home in Colorado, one of her neighbors shared with me that she had told her she was proud of me. It was good to know that she was after all the time that had passed. Even after all that happened with my parents, I believe that they are both in heaven, and I will see them again when I get there. There will only be love and peace there, and we will all experience the supreme love of God. When I talk about my parents now, I remember the good things and leave the bad out.

I think about the decision that my mother made about divorcing my biological father due to his gambling addiction and I wonder if she traded one trauma for another by marrying my stepfather. I wonder what the last straw was for her to make the decision about divorce. I also wonder if she would have known about the trauma that her children were going to suffer if a different decision had been made. I feel that when we find ourselves in a difficult situation, we find that our minds are in turmoil, and it becomes difficult to make a sound choice. I am not convinced that my mother relied on God in her younger years to help her through life's traumas that come our way. Trauma comes to us all in one way or another. In my own life, I heavily rely on the Lord to help me make the right decisions.

A Poem to My Mother

As I look back on the years passed, I see missed opportunities of reaching out to one another, A simple touch or word can mean so very much! I have always loved you but felt so far away from you at times. I know that the past has a lot to do with that. Thank God the past has been healed by the Masters hands! I love you (July 14, 2001).

A Brother Lost

When my brother Earl passed away, I had to take a 36-hour bus trip alone to Colorado to settle his affairs. When I first arrived at his apartment, two friends were there asking for the clothes they had left there. I let them gather their clothes, and after they had left, I did some cleaning. I tried to go through paperwork and get things in order as much as I could that night. It was after midnight before I drifted off to sleep. In the morning, I walked to the corner to get some coffee and something for breakfast. On my way there and back, I had to stop and vomit. The stress that I was feeling was overwhelming! I worked all day sorting, cleaning and packing. A neighbor of my brother's came over to take me to the funeral home to get his ashes, and I also went to see his social worker, that I had much contact with when she helped my brother. I thanked her for everything she did for him and wished her well. I also had to go to the police station to get a police report of what transpired with my brother's death. It was so sad to think that there was no one there with him when he died. But then I thought the Lord was there and was thankful for that. The neighbor, her husband and a friend of Earl's drove with me to a place in the mountains, and I found a beautiful meadow where we had a small service, and I said a prayer and then spread his ashes into the beautiful meadow in the mountains. My heart grieved, but I thought of all the times that me and Earl talked on the phone about the Lord, and I found peace that he wasn't struggling with an alcohol addiction any longer. He was finally at peace.

Changes Coming

I worked for a cleaning company in the evenings to be home with the children almost all day and up to bedtime. This way, at least one parent would be with the children, so we would not have to worry about childcare. We struggled with finances and always tried to make ends meet; God always provided what we needed.

When Tiffany was about 4 years old, and I was at work one night, cleaning, I was aggravated and talking to the Lord. Lord, is this all I am going to do? Is it clean, clean, clean? Suddenly, I heard a reply.... "NO, you will go to college and become a counselor. "I said, "Who's there?" I went and looked out the door of the room I was in, and there was no one. I looked to the left; I looked to the right, but there was no one. I realized it was the Lord speaking to me. Proverbs 4:25 Let your eyes look straight ahead; fix your gaze directly before you.

I asked Him what I would do with the boys, and He told me they would both be in school full-time. Before I could ask about Tiffany, He told me that HE would take care of her. There it was. I had to decide whether to obey the Lord's voice. I did.

It was one of the scariest times in my life as I walked through the doors of the college to register for classes and start a journey that would change my life. It had been 15 years since I graduated from High School. It was the Fall of 1996, and it took me 4 years to go part-time to accomplish an Associate of Arts degree. I felt such growth going on inside me intellectually.

I continued to work for the cleaning company during that time. One night, when I went to work, I told the company's owner that my van had been stolen. He was worried about how I was going to get to work. I told him that I was going to trust the Lord. He began to belittle me, and I became upset and began to cry. I went home that night after my shift and prayed to the Lord about it. Sometime later, while I was at work, my boss told me his van had been stolen. Deuteronomy 32:35 says Vengeance is mine, and recompense; their foot shall slip in due time; For the day of calamity is at hand and the things to hasten upon them. The Lord became my defender that night. I tried quitting this job several times, but the Lord told me no. I eventually applied for a Teller position at a bank where I had been cleaning and was hired. Because of this job, my husband and I could purchase a home. I worked for 9 years for that company.

Soon after I graduated with my associate degree, I got a full-time job at the Taylor Wal-Mart as a cashier. Four months later, I was promoted to the vision center and trained as an Optician. I thought it was wonderful to be trained as an optician. I even took a state exam to see if I could become a certified optician. The test was very difficult, and I could not pass the exam. I believe it was not the Lord's will for me to continue to be an Optician for my life's work. However, I still felt like I was doing something important with my life. I worked at Walmart while I continued my education.

Husband called to the Ministry

R obert had been called to the ministry, so I went through ministerial training with the Church of God in 2001. I spent about 15 months training with my husband. I had to do all the course work, attend all the classes, and participate in an internship with him. I thought the Lord was preparing us and would use us in a great way. Our thoughts are not His thoughts, and His ways are not ours (Isaiah 55:8-9). It wasn't until later I realized this. The months that we went through training were so exciting. We learned how to officiate a funeral, perform a wedding, do hospital visits, visit the sick, and minister to the needy. The task before us was sometimes tumultuous, but we worked together to finish the task. We hoped that Robert would be appointed to pastor a church and that we would see lives transformed and souls saved and made new in the power of Jesus Christ. Make no mistake, the enemy is right there trying to stop what God wants to do in our lives. We must stay vigilant because our adversary is a roaring lion seeking whom he may devour (1 Peter 5:8). No one is exempt from the traps that the enemy sets for us. We must stay close to the Lord no matter what; it is a matter of life, death, and an individual task. No one can do it for you, and you can't do it for someone else. We must be responsible people as we strive to follow the will of the Father in our lives. Just when you think all is well, the enemy strikes. May the God of Heaven help us all as we seek His face and righteousness.

Baker College Fall of 2005

I transferred the credits I had earned from Wayne County Community College (WCCC) and attended Baker College of Allen Park and earned my Human Service degree, and graduated Suma Cum Laude with a 3.99 GPA. Several staff there invested in me while I attended college, positively impacting my life.

I hadn't experienced that before, and it felt good. They took time to help me develop my resume so that I could begin applying for jobs in the Human Service field. While at Baker, I was awarded "Women's History Month Honoree, Empowering Through Service." I continued growing intellectually as well as spiritually in my life.

I was assisted with applying for a job in 2007 at The Senior Alliance (Area Agency on Aging TSA) in Western Wayne. I was hired and worked as a program specialist, and a year later, I was promoted to department manager. I oversaw all types of programs to help older adults in their homes. I couldn't believe I was working a professional job. I had come a long way in my education and still had a long way to go. I was overjoyed about what God was doing in my life.

I was sitting in class one day and wondered why I had gone through everything I had gone through, such as being on food stamps, welfare, having to be involved with Focus Hope for years, food pantries, and so forth. The Lord spoke to me in class, saying, "Now you will know how others feel when you refer them to these agencies."

Again, Romans 8:28 and we know that in all things, God works for the good of those who love him and have been called according to his purpose. Psalm 38:8 The Lord will fulfill his purpose for me; your love, O Lord, endures forever. Do not abandon the work of your hands.

While working at TSA, I won a contest twice at a 5-star hotel in Florida. I sold the most Holiday cards for $5.00, which would pay for a holiday meal delivered to a homebound senior on a specific holiday. One day, I stopped at a gas station and gave my talk about feeding seniors. I was told to go over to the window at the other end of the store and talk to the man behind the window. So, I did, and he yelled to the man at the register, "Give this woman $100.00!" That alone paid for 20 hot meals. The trips were beautiful. I went alone and had a wonderful time. It was a time of growth for me, and I loved every minute.

I also served on the advisory board for my friend Jaclyn for Michigan Paralyzed Veterans of America (MPVA) and received a service award. It was such an honor for me to receive this award. I loved being able to give myself to help others. Jaclyn was a good friend, and we still keep in contact through Facebook. I am proud of the young woman that she has become.

Inheritance Given

In 2006, we were left a large amount of money by a family friend named Gar, who had passed away. He had become good friends with our family and blessed us many times. He became the God Father to my daughter Tiffany when she was dedicated to the Lord.

With the money he left us, we fixed our roof and got new siding and gutters for our home, something we had needed to do for years. It looked great! We took our first real family vacation to Disney, got some things for our home and paid bills. Life was good!

I continued to take care of my family and worked a full-time job. Soon after we fixed the house, Robert lost his job due to plant closure. He was unemployed for 2 years; our home was foreclosed, and we moved to Belleville. I could not understand why God would allow us to get our home repaired finally, have our bills paid and have some extra, and then this happens. There was some more growing for me to do. You know, I needed to decide whether I was going to follow the Lord no matter what happened. I had to continually keep my eyes on the Lord to keep myself focused. I had to work my way through the grief I was feeling about the loss of our home.

I attended the University of Michigan in January 2008 and worked toward my bachelor's degree. I worked full-time at The Senior Alliance (TSA) and attended 2-3 classes a semester. I was extremely busy with work, attending classes, taking care of the children, doing the housework, and handling all the home responsibilities, and then there was all the homework that needed to be accomplished. I was driven to succeed.

Storm of Life

On May 15, 2009, my life changed drastically again, and I was sent into a whirlwind, what some would call "A PERFECT STORM." Psalm 119:71 It was good for me to be afflicted to learn your decrees. Psalm 118:13 I was pushed back and about to fall, but the Lord helped me.

I came home from the store to find a letter on the counter and all my husband's clothes were gone. He walked away and abandoned me without a single word. Psalm 94:17-19 Unless the Lord had given me help, I would soon have dwelt in the silence of death. When I said my foot was slipping, your love, O Lord, supported me. When anxiety was within me, your consolation brought joy to my soul.

I didn't know what to do. I was utterly devastated! How could this be happening to me? I was a Christian woman trying to live my life for the Lord. How could he do this to me and the children? My oldest son Robb was already living on his own, and Greg and Tiffany were still home. Tiffany was just 15 years old when this happened, and Greg was at a loss for what to think. He had always had a close relationship with his father, but something had changed along the way without him realizing it. The life I knew lay crumbled on the floor in a big heap. My heart had been ripped out, and I was bleeding profusely with no answers in sight. It was days before Robert contacted me.

I found out much later that my husband Robert had been discussing things with Tiffany and telling her things about me that were not true so he could get her on his side. My friend Jaclyn had told me something Tiffany had said to her while they were working at a fundraiser. Jaclyn had told me that Robert had been putting a lot of negative ideas about me in Tiffany's head and that Tiffany was very disenchanted with me because of what he was telling her. Jaclyn wasn't sure what to do or whether she should tell me. She eventually did.

One day, I saw that Tiffany had carved the word "fat" on her arm. I was devastated that she was doing this. I had studied about girls "cutting" themselves but had not experienced it with someone that I loved. When Robert came over one day around dinner time, I told him about it and asked him to stay for dinner so we could talk with her about it; he declined and left. Later, I discovered he had asked Tiffany to go with him for the weekend up north to see his mistress. I believe Tiffany was reacting the only way she could think of. How could he ask his 15-year-old daughter to go with him to visit his mistress? I can only imagine the turmoil that my daughter was experiencing in her own life. She had also struggled with many other things.

I stood in faith for my marriage for 16 months, no matter what the devil threw my way. I fought the battle, and I was bleeding. I filed for divorce from the husband that the Lord gave me and had been with for 28 years, 33 altogether. Ultimately, I surrendered everything to the Lord and put my entire family into the Lord's hands; that is where they are right now. I had to learn how to live without Robert and learn who Linda was.

2 Corinthians 10:4-5 The weapons we fight with are not the weapons of the world. On the contrary, they have the divine power to demolish strongholds. We demolish arguments and every pretension that sets itself up against the knowledge of God, and we take captive every thought to make it obedient to Christ.

Ephesians 6:12 For our struggle is not against flesh and blood, but against the rulers, against the authorities, against the powers of this dark world and the spiritual forces of evil in the heavenly realms. As I went through this very difficult, life-altering circumstance in my life, God's word became alive to me like never before! It's sharper than any double-edged sword (Hebrews 4:12).

So here I was once again. What was I going to do? I had to decide what to do.

I decided to begin counseling for the trauma I experienced in my life as a child in September of 2009, just 4 months after Robert left. I underwent intense group therapy with other women who had been traumatized by abuse in their lives. This is something I should have done years before this. I didn't know how before.

I could finally speak things out into the open and not be afraid of repercussions from anyone in the room. When I spoke out loud about what had happened to me as a child and even into my adult life, I found acceptance, understanding and compassion from the others in the room. Others had experienced the same abuse that I had experienced. I finally began to feel like I was going to make it, that I was going to be able to finally leave all the abuse and the evil I found myself in behind me. With God ALL things are possible (Mark 9:23).

I had mentioned to my counselor that I didn't know how I was making it through all the turmoil in my life (I know the Lord was present) and she responded, "When you were at school, you concentrated on school. When you were at home, you took care of the home. When you were at work, you took care of work." She was right!

Everyone needs to deal with their past and come to terms with it before God can use it to help other people. The little girl inside was growing up! Seven months had passed since Robert left, and I could finally tell my sisters and brothers what had happened. I shared it with them at a Christmas gathering. Robert's mom always supported me and couldn't understand how her son could do such a thing. Mom never turned her back on me but loved me even more. I have always compared our relationship with one another with

Ruth and Naomi. Ruth refused to leave her mother-in-law, and we refused to leave one another. Mom is such an important part of my life and always will be. She was a mother to me when my mother could not be. We talk with one another every day and hold one another in prayer. I have never known a woman as good as her. Her love is insurmountable.

Pressing Through

Matthew 9:20-22 talks about a woman with an issue of blood. I resonate with this story so much! For 12 years, she suffered and was alone. One day, this woman needed to decide to press through the crowd to get to Jesus. She tried everything else— she stepped out in faith because that is all she had. I am sure that she spent countless hours crying and wondering if her difficulties would ever get better. Just like this woman, all I had was my faith. So, I decided to press through all the garbage I had experienced to touch Jesus. I had to speak out loud the things that had me bound for so long— not only for the 12 years that the abuse went on but for my entire life.

When the Son sets you free, you are free indeed (John 8:32). Great healing took place in the following weeks, and I allowed him to go in and irrigate the unseen wounds. The healing took place from the inside out. The word of God talks about the Balm of Gilead. Is there no balm in Gilead? Is there no physician there? Why, then is there no healing for the wound of my people (Jeremiah 8:22)?

No matter what condition we are in or whatever despair or trouble we are going through, Jesus can heal our wounds and make us whole. God goes in where no one else can, and He performs the healing we desperately need. If we allow

Him, He will go into the darkest rooms where no one has been and clean out all the cobwebs, and then the light will shine in those places and ultimately bring victory.

Faith Increased

January 2010 - May 2010

I found myself on a cycle of destruction that I could not seem to get off as I watched my daughter being torn apart piece by piece. I am telling you this from a mother's heart and how it affected me. All I could do to combat the enemy was PRAY and PRAY I did! I prayed until I was completely exhausted. Then, I got into bed, got up the next morning, and went to work, day after day. My sweet girl was hospitalized 9 times in 5 months. She battled severe attacks from the enemy, and I experienced fear and uncertainty and was always on guard. My daughter struggled with bulimia, anorexia, depression, anxiety, cutting herself, suicidal ideation and attempts. Being her mother, I did not know how I was going to make it another day, and I didn't know how my precious daughter was going to survive all this torment. The enemy was relentless. Fear would grip me, and it would never let up. The more I prayed, the more I was attacked by fear. But God! Scripture states in Isaiah 43:2 When you pass through the waters, I will be with you; and when you pass through the rivers, they will not sweep over you. When you walk through the fire, you will not be burned, and the flames will not set you ablaze. Isaiah 48:10 Behold, I have refined you, but not with silver; I have tested you in the furnace of affliction (Isaiah 48:10). Through the trials I have gone through in my life, including this one with my precious daughter, God almighty was purifying me and removing all the dross in my heart so that He could see His reflection in me.

As a mother, I never imagined that my child would go through such traumatic things, and all that you can do is be supportive, love her and be there for everything... be there for it all. You can only do this with the Lord walking right next to you. You CAN NOT do this alone; I did not do this alone! The word of God tells us to pray without ceasing and to rejoice in all circumstances and so that is what I did (1 Thessalonians 5:16-18, James 1:2-3). We don't rejoice because of the circumstances but despite the circumstances. I received very little support from her father, and neither did Tiffany.

Listen to me closely, the devil is out to destroy us, our children and anything that matters to us. He will go through our children if he can't get to us. John 10:10 says: The thief comes to seek, kill and destroy; but the Lord says, I have come that they may have life, and have it to the full.

1 Peter 4:12-16 tells us [12] Dear friends, do not be surprised at the fiery ordeal that has come on you to test you, as though something strange was happening to you. [13] But rejoice inasmuch as you participate in the sufferings of Christ, so that you may be overjoyed when his glory is revealed. [14] If you are insulted because of the name of Christ, you are blessed, for the Spirit of glory and of God rests on you. [15] If

you suffer, it should not be as a murderer or thief or any other kind of criminal or even as a meddler. [16] However, if you suffer as a Christian, do not be ashamed, but praise God that you bear that name. I have learned from scripture that suffering produces perseverance (Romans 5:3). We decide what we will believe and do. Do we allow the enemy to have his way or the Lord to have His way in our lives?

More provisions from the Lord

I applied for and received a promotion in April 2010 to a larger department with a substantial pay increase. I had learned according to scripture about tithing, so I always ensured that I tithed my gross income to the Lord.

Psalm 75: 6-7 No one from the east or the west or from the desert can exalt a man. But it is God who judges, He brings one down, he exalts another. In the midst of my pain, God came in with a ray of sunshine. He gives us hope and a future to hold onto. My income was raised considerably so that all my needs would be handled. That is what God does.

Jeremiah 29:11 The Lord says, I know the plans I have for you, declares the Lord, plans to prosper and not to harm you, plans to give you hope and a future.

When I could not see my future, nor did I want to see my future.... God was unfolding it in front of my eyes. While working at TSA as the Information Services Manager in this new department, I became a certified Information Specialist, a certified Medicare/Medicaid Counselor, and a certified Care Transitions Coach, which prevented rehospitalizations within 30 days. The Bible tells us that if we need wisdom, ask God and he will give it to us liberally (James 1:5). These certifications were difficult, but I trusted God and He worked through me to accomplish these goals.

University of Michigan / Territory Enlarged

I transferred to the University of Michigan to work on my BA while continuing to work full-time and care for the family. When Robert left, I had just three semesters left until graduation. Several people told me I should put off school until things worked out with Robert and concentrate on that. I knew that if I had quit, I would have never finished what God told me to do. I knew that I had to finish the task before me. I believe that kept me going through all the turmoil in my life. It was difficult, but with God helping me, I knew I could succeed.

I had finally finished the course that the Lord had put me on back while I was working at the cleaning company. It was a difficult road that seemed impossible at times, but I continued toward the goal. There was a light at the end of the tunnel, and I graduated from the University of Michigan in 2009 with my BA in Psychology, Sociology, and Criminal Justice. As I walked into the graduation ceremony, my dreams were being realized, and the Lord unfolded it all for me.

God then called me to obtain my minister's license, so I submitted to the Lord and began the process. My pastor brought me before the Church to have me put forth in the ministry. I went through the Foundations course and the internship and received my Ordination for my Ministers License in 2015. I believed that I was obtaining my license to start my ministry to work with women who have been abused, but God had other plans for the time being. There was still work to be done for me.

Love Found Again

In December 2014, I began dating a man named Rick at church. We had a whirlwind romance, and we quickly fell in love. We had both been divorced for 12 years and each had three children. Rick was a retired police officer who treated me like a queen; I thought we would be together forever. I thought that the Lord had finally given me someone who would love me the way I needed to be loved. We spent a lot of time together going to places I had never been to. He went shopping with me once and helped me pick out clothes. Then, he waited while I tried them on and paid for them all. We talked about getting married and even looked at wedding rings. I was overjoyed. He once surprised me and took me to the shooting range where he helped me with shooting practice. It was so powerful as I shot the gun. I thought to myself how special this was due to him being a retired police officer and that he shared that part of his life with me.

The bishop called and asked me to fill a May pulpit in Jackson, MI. I was leaving for Florida because I had won my 2nd trip through work to a 5-star hotel in Florida, so I accepted the first two weeks of May 2015 and preached four services for those two Sundays. Afterward, I received a call again from the bishop asking me to consider becoming a Pastor. There were two churches to choose from, one in

Flint and one in Jackson, where I had preached. I explained that I would pray and let him know immediately. I wanted to decide before I left for Florida.

I prayed fervently, and the Lord gave me several scriptures telling me that was what He wanted. I called the bishop and told him I was accepting the church in Jackson, MI, and I began to be their pastor in July of that year. My life changed drastically as I began the daunting task of pastoring, and I would not be the same.

Rick and I continued dating while I prepared for the move, and I commuted to Jackson for services on Sundays and began ministering to the congregation. God grew me in insurmountable ways in the following months. I grew so much spiritually and prayed more than ever before in my life; the task was great! As I spent time in the Lord's presence, I became closer to Him in every way, and He directed me in everything I did. I was changing from the inside out and becoming more like Christ.

In August 2015, Rick broke it off with me by phone and told me he wanted to be friends. I was devastated and broken again in my spirit. Rick had scars that he needed to deal with in his life. I again began to live alone, moved into the parsonage in Jackson in October, and began looking for a job so that I would have medical insurance. I was hired at Thome PACE in March 2016 and continued working as a Pastor. This organization provides services to enable older adults to live in the community safely instead of in a nursing home. I started as an intake specialist and, about two years later, worked at the front desk as the staff chaplain for the seniors and the staff. Spiritual care for the seniors was dire because they were at the end of their lives. Working with these older adults is an honor, they have so much to give.

Because I was so busy, loneliness and depression seemed less present in my life. I heard years later from Rick's sister Lisa that Rick passed away and that he went home to the Lord. I was heartbroken but happy that he wasn't suffering any longer. I will never forget this man because I believe that the Lord gave us each other, even briefly, so that we both would know we could be loved again. I will see him again when I get to Heaven.

I poured myself into being the Pastor of New Life Worship and continued growing spiritually. I fell increasingly in love with Jesus as I sought him daily. The Lord cared for me and provided all my needs as I continued putting him first. He must be first. With the Lord's help, the congregation and I were able to make some improvements at the church. We got a new carpet in the basement, created a nursery, carpeted the children's church room, and applied a new coat of paint. Improvements were made to the sanctuary, and both the bathrooms were renovated. The Lord always provided what was needed for the improvements. I loved the people and longed to see God's hand move in their lives. The Holy Spirit had free reign in our service. People were saved and filled with the Holy Ghost, and their lives were transformed. We serve an awesome God that can do anything!

The Lord kept enlarging my territory, and I was also granted permission to do the books for the church. I became even busier. The Lord was surely preparing me for the future, and He knew that I would do whatever He wanted me to do and go wherever He wanted me to go.

Pandemic

A pandemic gripped the world, and everything was closed, including the church. The church doors were closed for 10 weeks, and Pastors everywhere began holding services virtually, including me. I had never done that before, but the Lord was growing me some more, and I continued to do so even after the doors were opened again. Because of the move of the Lord, my preaching became more powerful, and the Lord's anointing was falling on me. My prayer life was more fervent, and I depended on the Lord more and more. He is my love. This pandemic gripped people everywhere with fear. I refused to allow fear to control my life. Fear is the opposite of faith, and I knew that I needed my faith to rule over any fear that might come my way. There was a tremendous push for people to get a COVID-19 vaccination. I knew that this was not for me, so I applied for a religious exemption and was granted one. I believed that my immune system would care for me if I did get sick. People everywhere, whether they were vaccinated or not, got COVID-19. I got it twice and recovered fine from it.

Psalm 41:3 The Lord sustains them on their sickbed and restores them from their bed of illness. My trust is in the Lord of Heaven and Earth now and always.

New Beginnings

August 15, 2021
A story I shared in front of New Life Worship service

A woman went to have dinner with a friend named Kim. Kim began telling the woman about her summer plans, and she mentioned that she and her husband were going to Beaver Island to see a friend of theirs. Suddenly, God started talking through Kim that this friend was someone that the woman needed to meet. The woman said, "How?" And Kim told the woman she should come to the island with them.

Kim started talking so fast about how they would get the two of them to meet. Kim began texting her friend and asked for a picture, then Kim took a selfie of her and the woman and one of just the woman. Kim started texting her friend, and an hour later, her friend and the woman knew about each other.

The woman told her friend Kim that she would have to think and pray about whether she should make the trip to the island with them to meet this mysterious man.

Two days later, while the woman was reading her devotion, she read these words from the Lord, "All I require for you to do is take the next step, clinging to my hand for strength and direction" (Oswald Chambers devotional). The woman accepted the invitation and began holding God's hand. Kim provided the woman's phone number to the man, and text messages began the next day. After just two days, nightly phone calls began and after another 3 days, video chatting commenced.

God was unfolding a miracle, and it was all being done virtually. God spoke to this man concerning their relationship through a mysterious experience. One day, the man went to his office, and he found a painted rock, and on one side, it said: "This is just for you because Jesus loves you." On the other side, it said," Psalm 56:3 NIV When I am afraid, I put my trust in you. The man had no idea "who" put the rock there.

As these two individuals spent time together virtually, God began to unfold His will in their lives as God was binding them together. One day, while they were video chatting, the man asked about a chair that the woman was sitting in, and the woman told him that she had bought the chair from Kim some time ago. The man said, "Kim loaned that chair to me, and I sat and slept in it for several weeks." First, he sat in it, and then it was sold to the woman, and now it will have made a full circle. God knew it all the time!

Just twenty-seven days after Kim and the woman had dinner together, the man proposed marriage to the woman, and she accepted. This woman will change her name from Linda DeVore to Mrs. Linda Ann Miller. The ceremony will be on Beaver Island on September 4th, and they will begin their lives together with God, who will continue leading the way.

That gentleman, Steve Miller, has been worshiping with us this morning and is sitting right over there. With God, all things are possible. We serve an awesome God.

Only God could have put this all together. In just five short months, I met a man through mutual friends, got engaged, was married on Beaver Island and bought a beautiful home. I was standing in awe of what God was doing. Because we bought a home, the Lord released me from being the Pastor at New Life Worship. It was one of the most difficult things I have done because I loved being a pastor. I grieved over the decision but knew that God was taking me to another ministry level, and I needed to be obedient. I preached my last sermon at New Life Worship at the end of December 2021 and moved to Vermontville into a beautiful home that only the Lord could have given me and my husband, Steve. It truly is a miracle how it all came to pass; we bought the home from the mutual friends that introduced us! I had bought the wedding dress even before the proposal came.

We called the home "ANGEL HOME (Healing Our Minds Eternally). God was turning my vision that he gave me in college to work with women who have been sexually abused, and Steve will be working with men who are in crisis and addiction. We dedicated the home in honor of my dear friend Kathy Palmer, who has passed away and struggled her whole life with addiction. She is now in the presence of the Lord Almighty. There will be scholarships in her name to help others with their struggles. I always told Kathy that she would one day work with me, and now she would be. She will never be forgotten; her life mattered. She was the best friend I ever had. I could be myself, and she could be herself. Kathy is the only one I could share what happened to me in my childhood, making our relationship even more concrete. I accepted her for who she was, and she accepted me for who I was. We went through so many things together, and our friendship was like no other. Kathy was my daughter Tiffany's God mother, and they truly loved each other.

God made a way for Kathy to come from Florida and visit me at my home in Jackson before she passed away and was able to spend a week with me. My daughter Tiffany, granddaughter Scarlett, Kathy and I spent a whole day together at Sealife Aquarium at Great Lakes Crossing, and we had such a great time. God knew that He would take her home and gave us that gift before He did. I will forever be grateful to God for doing that for us. It had been over two years since I had been able to see her, and God provided as He always does. I am also thankful to her brother Dan and his wife Jan for providing Kathy with a visit.

Steve and I developed a mission statement for "Angel HOME. "

The mission of Angel Home is to raise public awareness of sexual abuse and offer its survivors the hope of eternal healing in mind, body and soul through the boundless resources of God's Holy Spirit.

Our Book of Life

I read once that our lives are like a book with many pages. We must read every line; nothing can be skipped, no matter what it conveys. Not every page will be pleasant, but it will be a part of us and can't be eliminated just because we want it to be. One day, I was asked to meet with the Executive Director, Social Worker and a patient who stated that he had problems with me. This patient had been very disruptive to several of the departments and caused problems with many people. He was a very intimidating man, and many were scared of him. As we sat at the table, this individual began talking and arguing. I sat there with my hands folded on the table and locked eyes with his man as he talked with the other two. In my mind, I began to say, "I rebuke you in the name of Jesus. I rebuke you in the name of Jesus." He kept looking at me in my eyes 'and then suddenly, he began to contradict himself while he talked. At the end of the meeting, we all stood, and as I approached the doorway, he bent down to me and said, "I know who you are, and you are a strong woman." I believe with all my heart that this was an evil spirit talking to me through this man. After this incident, he never caused problems with me again, and he soon disenrolled from the program. I will never forget this as I prayed for this man for deliverance in his life. God is stronger than any evil forces that we might encounter in our lives.

The unpleasant things that happen to us in our lives are what God uses to help others. We cannot empathize with others for something if we have not yet experienced it ourselves. Sympathy, yes, but not empathy. It is in the darkest hours of our lives that God shows up and shows us more of himself. Then, we become more like Jesus Christ and begin to emulate him more and more in our everyday life. I would not want to go back and rip out any page or anything that has happened to me in my life. You may ask, "Why?" The reason is that if I did that, I would not be the person that I am today. It has taken me a lifetime to get to know '" who" I am, and I like myself very much.

James 1:12 says Blessed is the one who perseveres under trial because, having stood the test, that person will receive the crown of life that the Lord has promised to those who love him. Again, Romans 5:3-5 says Not only so, but we also glory in our sufferings, because we know that *suffering produces perseverance;* **4** perseverance, character; and character, hope. **5** And hope does not put us to shame, because God's love has been poured out into our hearts through the Holy Spirit, who has been given to us.

I believe that everything that an individual goes through in this life can be turned around for good. Whether to quit or to push through and hold on until victory, a decision needs to be made. I look forward to the future and am excited about what the Lord of Heaven and Earth will do in my life and the lives of others. Love is the key to winning souls for the Lord; by spending time with Him anyone can accomplish great things for the Lord and win souls simultaneously.

My children continue to be of utmost importance in my life, and I continue to keep my three children and their families in the Lord's hands and pray that God will protect them from the enemy of their souls. I adamantly refuse to allow the devil to have his way in their lives. They all belong to God Almighty, and as long as I am their mother, I will continue to do so. I plead the blood of Jesus Christ upon them all. My son Robb has distanced himself from me and the rest of the family. I have not seen him, Angela or my beautiful grandson Antonio for about 4 years now. One thing that cannot be taken away from me is the freedom to pray, and I do for them all. We cannot change anyone, but only God can; when He does, there will be victory. The word of God tells us that He holds victory in store for the upright and guards the course of the just (Proverbs 2:7). He also says that His Word will not return void, but it will accomplish what He sets it out to do accomplish (Isaiah 55:11). We can trust His Word always!

Life Changed Yet Again

Life changes in an instant sometimes, and my life changes again. God surely had a plan for Steve and I and the home in Vermontville that He gave us. However, Steve allowed addiction to come in and steal everything that the Lord had given us. My heart was overwhelmed by the things that were happening in our lives. I had a difficult time sleeping and feeling safe. I prayed and fasted a lot and was at a loss about what I could do. We all make choices in our lives and live by those choices. I believed that the Lord had put us together for a reason and had a plan for our lives. Our enemy also has his plans, and he went to work immediately to destroy what God was trying to do in our lives. The thief comes to steal kill and destroy (John 10:10). The day after we got back from a beautiful honeymoon in Florida, the gavel dropped, so to speak. Steve came home very late, and when he came in, he cried uncontrollably. I asked him what was wrong, I thought that maybe someone had died. He kept crying, and within a few minutes, he confessed that he was gambling again and had withdrawn all the money from the account. I was heartbroken yet again. He had no answers as to why he did it. In the following months, I saw money taken from the account, and I asked him what the money was for. Steve became defensive and said he was putting money aside for a surprise for us in the fall. It was all a lie. He was

91

gambling. Lies and deception became rampant in everyday life.

Steve had not obtained an addictions counselor and refused to be accountable. He tried to be involved in bible studies, groups at church, reading scripture and writing in his journals. Acts 3:19 Repent, then, and turn to God, so that your sins may be wiped out, that times of refreshing may come from the Lord. Steve always repented but didn't turn away from the sin of gambling. I prayed that the Lord would give him the gift of the Holy Ghost to give him power from God. He would tell me about the Holy Ghost, "That is your experience." Acts 2:1-4 And when the day of Pentecost had fully come, they were all with one accord in one place.[2] And suddenly there came a sound from heaven like a rushing mighty wind, filling all the house where they were sitting. [3] And there appeared unto them cloven tongues like as of fire, and it sat upon each of them. [4] And they were all filled with the Holy Ghost and began to speak with other tongues, as the Spirit gave them utterance. I knew in my heart that Steve needed this power in his life. I felt that he was trying to be free from this addiction in his own power. He needed the power of the Holy Ghost.

I struggled with trusting Steve, and every time I thought I could, he gambled again, and the wounds became bigger. He continued to choose the addiction over me and what God wanted to do in our lives. I couldn't believe what he told me. I am sure he has a story about how this affected his life and will one day write his own book. I am on the other side of addiction. What I do understand is that addiction not only affects the one who is addicted, but it also affects everyone around them. I am expressing my feelings and my thoughts as his wife.

One time, when I arrived home from seeing my mom in Tennessee, Steve said that he "lost" his wedding ring and continued with how he might have done that. I looked at him, and immediately, the Holy Spirit told me, "He pawned it." His son and family arrived within 30 minutes for a weekend visit from the UP, so I had to keep it together while they were there. I had to act like everything was ok. Of course, Steve did also. I was so furious!

Fled for the Night

The next day, when they left for home and Steve went to work, I packed a bag and left and went to my friend Dawns home'. I left a note on the counter letting Steve know that I would be gone for the night but would return the next day. I had to get away to think and talk to God about what was happening. I was devastated again. Steve had his paycheck rerouted to his bank card, and then he gambled the entire paycheck away. This left us with no money for gas, food, or weekly bills. I didn't know what to do. I believe that he could not stop himself. He didn't know how not to gamble because he had done it for so long. He has told me that it gave him control over something. What he didn't realize was that he had no control.

While at my friend Dawn's home, I wrote down some things I needed to see Steve accomplish. He thought that we needed to deal with our relationship because he said that there were more problems than just his gambling in our marriage. What Steve could not see or understand because of the addiction was that because of his gambling, everything else hinged on that. This is not what I expected now that I was married again after being alone for 12 years.

He was unable to show any emotion about anything. He made me feel like I had to question everything I said or did.

Whenever he gambled, he would turn it all around on me and say what he thought I should be doing or why I wasn't doing it. My mind was in turmoil. I had to wear God's armor every day to protect myself against the enemy working through Steve.

Ephesians 6:10-18 [10] Finally, be strong in the Lord and his mighty power. [11] Put on the full armor of God so that you can take your stand against the devil's schemes. [12] For our struggle is not against flesh and blood, but against the rulers, against the authorities, against the powers of this dark world and the spiritual forces of evil in the heavenly realms. [13] Therefore put on the full armor of God, so that when the day of evil comes, you may be able to stand your ground, and after you have done everything, to stand. [14] Stand firm then, with the belt of truth buckled around your waist, with the breastplate of righteousness in place, [15] and with your feet fitted with the readiness that comes from the gospel of peace. [16] In addition to all this, take up the shield of faith, with which you can extinguish all the flaming arrows of the evil one. [17] Take the helmet of salvation and the sword of the Spirit, which is the word of God. [18] And pray in the Spirit on all occasions with all kinds of prayers and requests. With this in mind, be alert and always pray for all the Lord's people.

I often felt intimidated when I tried to talk to him about gambling. He didn't want to discuss it because he felt so bad about what he did. I felt oppression all around me, and I could feel the division between us. I felt intimidated. *I didn't know how to help him, so I prayed more.* Scripture addresses the spirit of intimidation, emphasizing that God doesn't give a spirit of fear but of power, love and self-discipline, encouraging believers to overcome intimidation through faith and reliance on God (2 Timothy 1:7).

Out of Work

Steve had two back surgeries and was out of work for quite some time, and we struggled with our bills. I had to apply for a grant through work to pay our mortgage and struggled to pay our monthly bills. I never felt like I got caught up. I constantly took from Peter to give to Paul, so to speak. I thought, "When will this get better? "

Old feelings began to creep in as if I was not good enough. I felt unloved by him and unwanted. I worked hard around the house trying to maintain it. Again, it was a 3 thousand square foot home. Once when we were in the kitchen, he told me that he made three quarters of the money and needed to have money to "live on." When he said that, I felt like I wasn't doing enough. We purchased this home with my retirement, and I also took out a loan to get what we needed. There was a great strain on our marriage, so I prayed more. The Bible tells us to pray without ceasing (1 Thessalonians 5).

I wanted us to use this home for God's glory and make a difference in other people's lives. We looked at the possibility of fostering and setting up appointments to obtain more information. However, as time passed, I saw no way to do this when there was utter turmoil in the home. I sought the Lord and prayed over Steve for deliverance once and for all. The word of God tells me that when the Son sets you free, you are free indeed (John 8:36). I had a past and had been delivered from it. How come it wasn't the same for Steve? Only God knew. Steve told me several times that he has left a trail of destruction in his life. That was so true! Nothing seemed to help him to change. I don't share these things to hurt Steve, he is my husband and I love him. I share them to show what addiction can do, any addiction that people struggle with. There are many people struggling with addiction.

I told Steve that I needed to take his name off the main account, so I made an appointment, and he signed the paperwork to remove his name. The Gambling didn't cease.

A few of our friends agreed to be accountability partners for Steve and agreed to meet at our home bi-weekly. This only lasted, I believe, for three meetings because when the conversation got too heated, Steve would walk out of the room. I never would have thought I would be in such a situation. My income alone was not enough to pay all the bills, as we also needed Steve's income. I experienced being abused emotionally, psychologically and financially. He never abused me physically.

One night, as I was sleeping, suddenly, I felt like something had passed over me, and it startled me awake. I felt like there was an evil spirit lurking around. Not realizing it, these spirits entered our home. I had to depend on the word of

God if I would make it through all this. I had to anoint the home and pray several times.

One day, I sat down with Steve to talk about the situation that we were in financially. I explained that if I didn't see things change, I would put the house up for sale, file for a legal separation, and sell things to pay the bills. I also told him I loved him and wanted our marriage to be saved.

Things went well for about a week; we prayed together and sang in the prayer room upstairs. I had hope but was soon dashed again, so I contacted a realtor and put the house up for sale the next day. I had a yard sale, sold what I could, gave things away, and purged what I could to prepare for the move. I had to contact my church family for assistance with the mortgage payment and the consumer's bill. It had to be paid, or it would have been detrimental to my credit; I had worked for over 12 years to heal my credit report. My church, New Hope in Charlotte, helped me with the mortgage for September and the Consumer's bill. Alone and with God's help, I paid all the bills for August through October. The only way I know I could do this is because I continued to give my tithes first. When we put God first, his word promises to prevent the devourer from devouring our crops (Malachi 3:11).

The house was sold within 30 days, and the closing was set for us to sign the paperwork. Promises were made but never kept. Without the Lord, I would never have survived this tumultuous time. God tells us in Proverbs 6:30-31 [30] Men do not despise a thief if he steals to satisfy his soul when he is hungry; [31] But if he be found, he shall restore sevenfold; he shall give all the substance of his house. Sevenfold refers to full, complete, and perfect payback or compensation.

Preparing for the Future

Ipacked up the house, and with the help of my pastor and a friend at church, I moved my belongings into a storage unit and only kept the necessities with me. I had nowhere to go, so I lived with my friend Dawn and her husband Vern for about 4 months. I looked for somewhere to live, and Steve found himself an apartment. Dawn and Vern were godsends to me. I wasn't charged any rent to live there or asked to pay any bills, but I helped with groceries as often as possible. I was in a safe haven. I had come down with COVID while there, and Dawn took care of me. She was a real friend to me when I needed her the most. I prayed and fasted often, sometimes for 5 days at a time, to hear from God.

Steve and I had very little contact during that time. I searched for an apartment or house for sale or rent. However, I wasn't making enough money for the ones I found. Every area of my life was affected during this time. My marriage, home, work, finances, and health. I believe that the stress that I was under had to manifest in some way, and it did. I severely itched all over my body. I saw the doctor twice and the dermatologist. The enemy was trying to destroy me like he had always tried. I had news for him: nothing would deter me from trusting Jesus Christ in my life, and he was messing with the wrong person. I only became stronger because of the trials I faced. The word of God tells me that suffering produces perseverance. Again, Romans 5:3-5 NIV ³ Not only so, but we also glory in our sufferings, because we know that suffering produces perseverance; ⁴ perseverance, character; and character, hope. ⁵ And hope does not put us to shame because God's love has been poured out into our hearts through the Holy Spirit, who has been given to us.

I was scheduled to sign paperwork for an apartment in Jackson that Dawn had helped me find; it was very small, about 500 square feet. I would have to get rid of even more belongings. I had already lost so much! Steve told me about a different apartment, so I immediately filled out an application. I was accepted and moved into a two-bedroom apartment in Jackson. I told him that God used him to help me to find a bigger apartment.

Little Contact

Over the next 9 months, Steve and I had some contact and tried to work things out. Steve had a way of reeling me back in. I felt like I was in turmoil the way things were going in my life. I could not understand "why" things were the way they were. We attended church together, and he said he wanted a water baptism. Hope sprung up within me as I assisted the pastor in baptizing him. I believed that things would change. However, things got even worse. I believe the enemy went full force, trying to destroy what God was trying to do. I eventually told Steve that we needed to not see each other for now so that he could work on getting an addictions counselor and concentrate on his relationship with God. My mind was overwhelmed, and I didn't know what to do again. I blocked him on my phone, and he showed up at my door two hours later. Again, he reeled me back in.

I fasted for 5 days without food, praying and seeking the Lord for him. The Lord gave me scripture, and I was in tune with God's voice. I rebuked and named the evil spirits that seemed to control Steve in his life. I was in spiritual warfare for Steve, and the enemy knew it. The next day, Steve told me that he had vomited severely and didn't know why. I believe that he vomited the evil spirits out. When Steve left the pastorate after his first divorce, he went into addiction rather than seeking the Lord. The word of God tells us in

Matthew 12:43-45 [43] "When an impure spirit comes out of a person, it goes through arid places seeking rest and does not find it. [44] Then it says, 'I will return to the house I left.' When it arrives, it finds the house unoccupied, swept clean and put in order. [45] Then it takes seven other spirits more wicked than itself, and they go in and live there. And the final condition of that person is worse than the first. That is how it will be with this wicked generation." I believe this is what happened to Steve.

Last Straw

I decided that for my mental health and well-being, I had to separate myself from Steve. I was leaving for Tennessee the next morning, so I prepared a voice text for Steve and sent it to him just before leaving for Tennessee for 5 days. I explained to him that I was done with our marriage, that I was blocking him on my phone and to not show up at my door, and that if he did, I would call the police. I assured him I would continue to pray for him and hope for the best in his future. I also sent the message to my friend Kim so that when Steve contacted her, she would know what was happening. I asked her not to be a go-between when Steve asked her to do so to get to me. I felt relieved as I was driving to Tennessee to see mom. I thought to myself that I can finally begin healing from all this turmoil. I grieved at what could have been and what I had hoped for as I began the healing process. I have experienced that every time something detrimental happened in my life, I had two choices. I could either become despondent, or I could become a stronger individual. I always chose to become stronger with the help of Jesus Christ. I decided to see a counselor so that I could work through all that had happened to me in this marriage. I believe it was imperative to do this so that it all could be dealt with and put to rest in my mind and heart before I could move on. Many tears were shed and lessons learned as I sought the Lord in my life.

One of my favorite scriptures is Isaiah 41:10 So do not fear, for I am with you; do not be dismayed, for I am your God, I will strengthen you and help you; I will uphold you with my righteous right hand. With Christ by my side, I will always be victorious.

Preparing for the Future

I had lived in the apartment that I rented for about 9 months, so I contemplated whether I should stay there or start looking for a home to buy. I prayed and began to look around at my options.

I received a letter regarding my school loans, which I had been paying for 10 years. I was enrolled in a program that entailed working for a non-profit for 10 years, and when that was accomplished, the school loans were satisfied. I had finally reached this threshold, and the letter I received stated that no more payments were required and that all had been satisfied. What a tremendous relief this was to me in my life. Such a burden was lifted off my mind and heart! This increased my credit score greatly. I also received another raise at work and made a good income.

My sister Elinore and her husband Terry were in the process of moving back to Michigan from South Carolina and had looked at several homes. They found a manufactured home community and bought a brand new one. There were also a couple of other homes for sale in the community, so I decided to tour the homes and see if this was where I was supposed to buy a home or not. After I toured the homes and prayed, I decided to put an offer in on one of the homes. I came down from the asking price, and it was countered. I agreed and accepted, signed the paperwork and prepared to move into my new home. I still had three months on my lease at my apartment, so I wrote a letter to the management to see if they would let me out of my lease. They let me out of my lease and sent me a check with the security deposit I paid when I moved in. God is so good to me.

Again, my church family and some close friends helped me move from Jackson to Belleville, and I moved in on August 26. There is nothing that compares to a church family in this life. They helped me move everything and placed all my belongings in my new home. My church family drove 45 minutes to my apartment, loaded the truck, drove an hour to my new residence, unloaded the truck, and then drove an hour and a half to their homes. I will never forget the love they showed me in my life. I was sad because I had to find a new church family. After all, it's an hour and a half drive to church, which is unfeasible to do and be involved like I wanted to be. I unpacked everything and put it away within two days, except the wall hangings. I was trying to get things accomplished before I had to have a double surgery that was scheduled for September 20th. I was initially supposed to have the surgeries on September 1st, but the surgeons postponed them until September 20th. I believe the Lord had something to do with this so I could get all settled in before the surgeries.

My friend Dawn took me to the hospital on the day of surgery and stayed until I came out of surgery. I had to have hysterectomy and bladder surgery. Two days later, there were complications, and I was taken back for a 3rd surgery due to a large hematoma that had developed. What was supposed to be an overnight stay turned into a 4-day hospital stay? Once discharged home, my friend Dawn and my sister Mary took me home and got me settled. My sister Mary stayed with me for a few days because I was worried about being alone.

By September 29th, I became severely constipated; I believe it was due to the pain meds I was taking. I tried everything to alleviate this, but nothing helped. I ended up calling 911 and went by ambulance to the ER. After waiting 8 hours in the ER and in severe pain, I was seen. The Dr. did a cat scan, and it revealed that the bladder was enlarged, which caused a UTI, and there were feces everywhere. I was given a leg Cath to relieve the pressure on the bladder, which I had just had surgery on. During my time in the ER, I often had to make my way down the hall to the bathroom.

I was in absolute dire need. I still see myself clutching the back of my hospital gown and trying to walk as fast as possible to the restroom with tears streaming down my face and crying out to the Lord for help. I knew He was present and that I would indeed get through this. Later, I was discharged, and my daughter Tiffany picked me up, took me home, and settled me. I was given an antibiotic and that stuff you must drink when you get a colonoscopy. Over the next two days, I drank that stuff and prayed that I would make it to the bathroom in time. I was home alone and very weak. As I was in the ER, there was a lady there, and she was telling me that she had just been diagnosed with pancreatic cancer and was in severe pain. I talked with her about heaven, and she said, "I hope I go there." I explained to her that she could be sure and told her how she could be. Her eyes lit up, and she seemed more at peace as we talked. This lady decided to go home, thanked me, and told me she would be praying for me. Amid our pain, God uses us in the direst situations of life, and when He does that, we know that it is Him doing the work and that HE receives the glory for it. I know that I will see this lady in heaven one day.

I read a quote from Oswald Chambers: We are not made for the mountains, sunrises or other beautiful attractions of life. Those are to be moments of inspiration. We are made for the valley and the ordinary things of life, and that is where we are to prove our stamina and strength. I know that it is in the valley that we are made to be more like Christ. We must reach the point in life that when we are taken to the valley, we know in our hearts it is for our benefit and that the Lord Jesus is right there with us through it all, giving us the strength to prevail.

On October 1st, my hematoma began bleeding profusely, and I could not get it to stop. I had a post-op appointment scheduled for the 3rd, but it was worrying me that I could not get it to stop bleeding. I called the doctor's office on October 2nd and decided to drive to the ER in Jackson, an hour away. Once I arrived, I was taken care of very well. A test was taken to see if I could urinate by myself so that the Cath could be taken out. I was able to do so and was relieved of the cath. A few more strips were applied to the wound, and the bandage was applied. I was taken all the way out to my car by wheelchair and drove the hour home. I drove to Jackson again the next day to follow up with my surgeon, who did a bladder scan, and all was well. He was concerned about the wound, so he asked me to follow up again with him at the end of the month. I felt like I was finally beginning to heal from this traumatic event in my life. God's word says that when we are weak, He is made strong (2 Corinthians 12:9-10). I had just two more weeks before I could return to work and was glad to do so. I work full-time for the PACE Program (Program for All-Inclusive Care for the Elderly). I am the staff Chaplain for approximately 300 older adults and also staff at Huron Valley PACE in Ypsilanti. I minister to the spiritual needs of these individuals.

Submission to God

The Lord was dealing with me about restoration with Steve. I fought this for some time, remembering what I had been through with him in the past. I went back and forth about it. I prayed and fasted about it and talked to the Lord about it. At the time, I could not believe that God was working in this way in my life. I didn't want to do it! However, I submitted to what God was doing and asking of me. I contacted Steve to see if he would consider restoration. He said that he would pray about it and get back with me. About 5 days later he contacted me and said that he was willing. If I could have seen what the future held for us, I probably would not have agreed to restoration. That would have been disobedience, and the word of God tells me that disobedience is like witchcraft. 1 Samuel 15:23 For rebellion is like the sin of divination, and arrogance like the evil of idolatry. The only right choice was to follow what the Lord was asking me to do. I needed to walk by faith and not sight (2 Corinthians 5:7). In December of 2023 he moved in with me to the home that I bought, and we began the tumultuous task of restoration.

Within 2 months, he was gambling again. Tears flowed from my eyes often and I wondered why God allowed this trial in my life. Scripture says in Psalm 56:8 You keep track of all my sorrows. You have collected all my tears in a bottle. You have recorded each one in Your book. The enemy was relentless and was trying to destroy Steve and our marriage. He was always sorry, but things didn't change. He had been struggling with this addiction now for about 15 years. There was nothing that I could do but pray and I did.

Oswald Chambers said, "just because I don't understand what Jesus Christ says, I have no right to determine that he must be mistaken in what he says. That is a dangerous view, and it is never right to think that my obedience to God's directive will bring dishonor to Jesus. The only thing that will bring dishonor is not obeying him. I know when the instructions come from God because of their quiet persistence. Faithfulness to Jesus means that I must step out even or when I can't see anything. Faith is a deliberate commitment to the Person of Jesus Christ even when I can't see the way ahead. Whatever He says to you do it."

This is how I felt, and I knew in my heart that I needed to be obedient. Even as I write this, I still think about ending this marriage, but I know that God is able to do far and above all that I can hope or imagine. We decided that counseling was needed, and so we went to see a marriage counselor. After many sessions, the couple that we saw said that they needed to refer us to other counselors due to the severity of our situation. I scheduled with a counselor alone and Steve ended up not seeing anyone.

Isaiah 24:15 Glorify the Lord in the Fires. We are to honor the Lord *in* the trial… *in* the very thing that afflicts us.

Although there are examples where God did not allow His saints to even feel the fire, usually the fire causes pain. It is precisely there in the heat of the fire we are to glorify Him. We do this by exercising perfect faith in His goodness and love that has permitted this trial to come upon us. Even more we are to believe that out of the fire will arise something more worthy of praise than had we never experienced it. Many might say: You must retreat to the world's ways of acting. It is too difficult for you to continue living the part of a Christian. Abandon your principles. Yet no matter how much Satan may pressure me to follow his course, I cannot for I am a child of God. The Lord's divine decree has commanded me to go from "strength to strength" (psalm 84:7). Therefore, I will, and neither death nor hell will turn me from my course. And if for a season He calls me to "stand firm," I will acknowledge it as time to renew my strength for greater strides in the future. In times of uncertainty- wait. If you have any doubt- wait, never forcing yourself into action. If you sense any restraint in your spirit, do not go against it- wait until the way is clear (L.B. Cowman from Streams in the Desert).

The Man

Steve is an intelligent man. He graduated from Seminary, was a Pastor for 24 years, and now works as a Hospice Chaplain. He dabbles in painting and crochets, is a good cook, draws and sings wonderfully, and has many other interests. I sometimes see the "Real" Steve, gentle and loving. But when he gambles, he is someone different. He regresses into himself and never wants to talk about it. It gets swept under the rug and turns it around on me and what I am doing wrong.

My heart was in turmoil, and the only thing I could do was seek the Lord. I spent a lot of time in secret prayer in the prayer closet. Matthew 6:6 when you pray, go into your room, close the door and pray to your unseen Father. Then your Father, who sees what is done secretly, will reward you. I had to be close to the Lord for His strength to be in my life. The word of God says in 2 Corinthians 12:10 For when I am weak, then I am made strong. The Lord had me in the fire of affliction and refining me. It is a difficult process. He was removing the chaff (worthless things) from my life. God can only improve us by allowing trials and tribulations to enter our lives. We do not grow on the mountains when all is good and beautiful. When we are in the valley of sorrow and difficulty, we grow in the valley and our lives improve.

Steve received a lump sum from his retirement, and we were able to add a new deck to the back of the house. My brother-in-law Terry did the work, and we assisted him. It looks good, and we are enjoying it. I would go to work and feel more like myself, but when I got home, I was on guard. Trust was nonexistent, and I didn't know if I could trust him again. I know that Steve was struggling emotionally, psychologically and even spiritually, but I could not do what was needed; only he could, and that was to seek the Lord. Scripture says in Jeremiah 29:11-13 [11,] " I know the plans I have for you," declares the Lord, "plans to prosper you and not to harm you, plans to give you hope and a future. [12] Then you will call on me and come and pray to me, and I will listen to you. [13] You will seek me and find me when you seek me *with all your heart.* God had something amazing for both of us, but the enemy was trying to stop it. Again, I know the Lord Jesus is omnipotent, omniscient, omnipresent (all-powerful, all-knowing and everywhere present), and I must continue to trust Him and His timing. He is never too late or too early; He is right on time.

I could not understand "Why" God was allowing this in our lives. I shared things with a couple of dear friends who prayed for me. I kept it from my family because when God gives us something that seems unfair or impossible to overcome, I knew that I needed to keep my circle of influence small so that I would not be deterred from what God required from me. 1 Corinthians 15:57 says, thanks be to God, who gives us the victory through our Lord Jesus Christ. The word of God says that when you have done all that you can do, stand (Ephesians chapter 6).

We picked out new furniture for the house, and I ended up paying it off when I sold my old car. We went on a cruise and had new countertops, and a dishwasher installed, and we are still paying it off. These things were supposed to be paid for with his retirement. Finances were strained, and I am doing my best to pay for things on time. My credit has been affected, and I am trying to get it back in order.

In Crisis

Steve told me that he was going to retire and that he was in crisis. He was having difficulty doing his job. His mind needed to be rewired due to years of gambling addiction. I hardly recognized the person sitting in the chair next to me. I wanted to discuss this because if he retired, he would not have medical insurance anymore, and our finances would be in worse shape. He had already made up his mind. He said that he was going to work a part-time job and that he had a monthly retirement that he would get. He was getting one more check; I would use it to pay bills. However, he got off work, drove 2 hours to a casino in Grand Rapids, and gambled his whole paycheck! I told Steve that something had to change! He said he would reroute his part-time job and retirement to my account and that he is tired of living this way. He is entering counseling, attending Gamblers Anonymous (GA) meetings, beginning counseling, and seeking the Lord with all he has. He wrote up a two-page declaration of what he was going to do.

Psalm 13:1-2, 5-6 How long, Lord? Will you forget me forever? How long will you hide your face from me [2] How long must I wrestle with my thoughts and have sorrow in my heart day after day? But I trust in your unfailing love, and my heart rejoices in your salvation [6] I will sing the Lord's praise, for he has been good to me.

My heart was so broken, and I knew that only God could repair the brokenness. I know that God will take care of me no matter what happens. He always has and always will. He is my best friend, and I love Him wholeheartedly.

I have shared with Steve that I will no longer be enabling him. I set boundaries and allowed him to feel the consequences of his gambling. Codependency can lead to feelings of resentment, exhaustion, and helplessness. I have felt trapped in a cycle that I can't escape. Trying to manage the effects of the addiction has been consuming and frustrating. I feel like, at my age, I should be at a more stable time in my life. Unless you have lived with a spouse who has an addiction, a person does not know what they would do in this situation. All I know is that I must obey when God leads me to do something. Only God knows if Steve will come out on the other side of this trial in his life. I must decrease, and God must increase in my life (John 3:30). I hope that we both come out on the other side of this addiction and will allow God to use it all to bring Him glory. Many in this world are affected by addiction, and if Steve and I can help some of them find hope, then it will all have been worth the pain. The fire has been hot, but I know it has a purpose, and I must submit to it. It does not matter what anyone says about it or me. It only matters what God says about me and what He thinks of me, for who knows but that I have been brought to this position for such a time as this (Esther 4:14).

I trust God in the situation that I am in right now with my husband and the gambling addiction that not only affects him but me as well as his wife. I could have made the decision to end the marriage, but God had other plans. I must obey what God leads me to do in my life and in my marriage. We made a covenant before God and that covenant is a solemn commitment of faithfulness not only to God but to the husband that I married. It was for the good times and the bad times as well. In sickness and in health until death do us part. I must cast all my fears and worries onto the Lord and let Him carry them (1Peter 5:7). Why? Because He will never fail, and He is the One that can touch my husband's heart and change it and then I will see victory over addiction in his life. It is through Gods power that addiction can be broken, not by anything that we can do, but only God. I am standing in the gap for my husband, and I hope that if it was me, he would do the same (Matthew 19:6, Mark 10:9).

Blessings Received

Throughout my life, there have been blessings from the Lord provided for me. One time, when my first husband Robert and I were going to be evicted from our apartment the very next day, we went to church and went up to the altar for prayer. No one knew the need, but after prayer, people approached us in our seats and began putting money into our hands. One man put a large roll of money in my hand, and I knew it had to be his entire paycheck. When we left the church that day, we had enough money to pay our rent in full and for other needs. God is always on time. His word declares in Psalm 50:10 for every animal of the forest is mine, and the cattle on a thousand hills. Also, in Haggai 2:8 The silver is mine, and the gold is mine, declares the Lord Almighty. Everything belongs to the Lord, and we can never out-give Him. When we put Him first in everything, even our finances, He promises to take care of us. There have been many beautiful trips taken, cruises enjoyed at many destinations, money provided on many occasions, promotions given, checks received in the mail, bills paid, and needs provided in ways that cannot be explained except that we serve an awesome God that takes good care of us. The God I serve hears me when I pray as He does others when they pray. He hears us, answers us and provides for us. There is no other God that does that.

Scripture declares in John 14:6 Jesus answered, "I am the way and the truth and the life. No one comes to the Father except through me. He is the door we need to go through (John 10:9). Jesus made a way when there was no way. Do you believe that today? I pray that you do.

Many things happened to me in my life that I thought were terrible. I have survived many traumas in my life, but God turned all those things around that were meant for evil and turned them into something good (Genesis 50:20). We can't go back and change anything in our lives, and we can only go forward and allow God to use whatever He wishes to bring Him glory. He deserves all Glory for everything.

Victory Promised

G od gave me the vision of H. O. M. E. while I was in college, and it stood for (Healing Our Minds Entirely). When Steve and I moved into the home in Vermontville, I allowed it to be called "Angel HOME" (Healing Our Minds Eternally). I have repented to God for changing what He gave me so long ago, and I am again calling it what He decided to call H.O.M.E. (Healing Our Minds Entirely). It will be an organization that will help other women to heal from every form of abuse in their lives and help them allow God to turn it all around in their lives to bring Him glory. This book is the first step in that process for me. God will surely lay out the details for me as I move along the continuum in the life God gave me. My life belongs to Him, and to Him be the glory. He has been working on me my entire life to prepare me for what He has for me. He is still working on me, and I am grateful for that.

I look forward to the future and believe in God for things beyond my capabilities. Jeremiah 33:3 NIV says [3] Call to me, and I will answer you and tell you great and unsearchable things you do not know. I am dreaming for big things in my life, and I know that God is able to fulfill those dreams.

Psalm 30: 11-12 You turned my wailing into dancing, you removed my sackcloth and clothed me with joy that my heart may sing to you and not be silent. O Lord my God, I will give you thanks forever. Psalm 34:18-19 The Lord is close to the broken hearted and saves those who are crushed in spirit. A righteous man may have many troubles, BUT the Lord delivers him from them ALL.

The Lord gave me the following scripture when He called me to school so I created my email account with it so that I would never forget it: Hebrew 10:35-36 So do not throw away your confidence, it will be richly rewarded. You need to persevere so that when you have done the will of God, you will receive what he has promised. It wasn't until years later that I learned that perseverance didn't come without first suffering.

Maybe you have been holding onto something that no one else knows about, something that you have been hiding, protecting yourself from. The Lord is able to set you free from what you have been holding onto. We don't have to protect ourselves; God is our protector. Put it in HIS hands today and see what the Lord will do.

For years, I wanted someone to love me and experience a love beyond comprehension. There is no greater love than the love of the Father. His love is complete, all-consuming, unconditional, never-ending and a love that is like no other. He was present throughout my life, loving and caring for me in all circumstances. He was preparing me for something greater than myself. He is more than enough for me. He is the first in my life, and no one will take His place. I am willing to do whatever He wants me to because He knows what is best for me.

God's word tells us that his thoughts are not our thoughts nor our ways (Isaiah 55:8-9). Lay your life into His capable hands and know that He will never fail you even in the most difficult times in your life. He is our advocate (1 John 2:1).

Take the first step and submit your life to Him. When we repent and ask God to forgive us of our sins, we are born again into the family of God, and we are His. He then begins to turn everything around for our good. Allow Him to do whatever He chooses, and rest knowing that it is in your best interests even when you may not understand. It will be a wonderful story of hardships turned into victories, sadness turned into unspeakable joy and a life that the Master of the Universe will fashion. Don't delay another minute, pray to the Father in heaven, He is waiting to hear from you. John 15:16 16 You did not choose me, but I chose you and appointed you so that you might go and bear fruit—fruit that will last—and so that whatever you ask in my name the Father, I will give you. May God bless you as you move forward in your book of life. God will be with you every step of the way, and you will see many wonderful things along the way. May each young lady that looks into a mirror see the reflection of the Lord Jesus Christ looking back at them and then the little girl that once was there will have experienced great healing in her life and will never be the same and knowing without a doubt that whatever comes your way, you will make it through any difficulty that may arise. In Jesus name, I pray, Amen.

May God bless all the little girls richly as He alone brings healing to all you have been through, and it will bring Him glory.

References

Holy Bible King James Version

Holy Bible New International Version

Oswald Chambers, My Utmost For His Highest, 1992 by Oswald Chambers Publications, Original Edition 1935 by Dodd, Mead and Company, Inc. Copyright renewed 1963 by the Oswald Chambers Publication Association, Ltd, All rights reserved.

Streams in the Desert, Copyright 1925, 1953, and 1965 by Cowman Publications, Inc., and copyright 1996 by Zondervan Association, Ltd.

The Complete Works of E. M. Bounds on Prayer, Compilation 1990 by Baker Books, Forward 2004 by Jim Cymbala

.

www.ingramcontent.com/pod-product-compliance
Lightning Source LLC
Chambersburg PA
CBHW051530120626
46551CB00012B/1156